Usborne
First hundred words
in Russian

Heather Amery

Illustrated by Stephen Cartwright

Russian language consultant: Katerina Burgess
Edited by Jenny Tyler and Mairi Mackinnon
Designed by Mike Olley and Holly Lamont

 There is a little yellow duck to find in every picture.

СТИНАЯ   *gasteenaya*   The living room

папа
***pa**pa*   Daddy

мама
***ma**ma*   Mummy

мальчик
***mal'**chik*   boy

девочка
dyevachka　girl

ребёнок
ribyawnak　baby

собака
sabaka　dog

кошка
koshka　cat

3

Одежда

adyezhda Clothes

обувь
*o**boof'*** shoes

трусы
*troo**sy*** pants

джемпер
*****djem***pir* jumper

4

майка
*mai*ka vest

брюки
bryooki trousers

футболка
*foot***bol**ka t-shirt

носки
*nas***kee** socks

5

Кухня

koohnya The kitchen

хлеб
hlyep bread

молоко
malako milk

яйца
yaytsa eggs

яблоко

ya*blaka*   apple

апельсин

*apil'****seen***   orange

банан

*ba****nan***   banana

Мытьё посуды

myt'yo pasoody   Washing up

стол
stol   table

стул
stool   chair

тарелка
*tar**yel**ka*   plate

8

НОЖ
nosh knife

ВИЛКА
veelka fork

ЛОЖКА
loshka spoon

КРУЖКА
krooshka cup

Игрушки  *igrooshki* Toys

лошадь
*lo*shat' horse

овца
aftsa sheep

корова
*karo*va cow

курица
*koo*ritsa   hen

свинья
sveen'ya   pig

поезд
*po*yest   train

кубики
*koo*biki   bricks

В гостях   *v gastiah*   On a visit

бабушка
***ba**booshka*   Granny

дедушка
***dye**dooshka*   Grandpa

тапочки
***ta**pachki*   slippers

пальто
pal'to coat

платье
*pla*t'ye dress

шапка
*shap*ka hat

Парк

park   The park

дерево
*d**ye**riva*   tree

цветок
*tsvye**tok***   flower

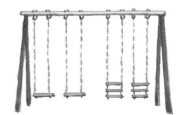

качели
*ka**chye**lee*   swings

мяч
myach   ball

детская горка

*dyetskaya **gor**ka*   slide

сапоги

*sapa**gee***   boots

птица

***ptee**tsa*   bird

лодка

***lot**ka*   boat

Улица

oolitsa   The street

машина
masheena   car

велосипед
vilasipyet   bicycle

самолёт
samalyot   plane

грузовик
*grooza**veek*** truck

автобус
*af**taw**boos* bus

ДОМ
dom house

17

Вечеринка

vichireenka   The party

воздушный шар
vazdooshniy shar   balloon

торт
tort   cake

часы
chasy   clock

18

мороженое
marozhenaye ice cream

рыба
ryba fish

печенье
pichen'ye biscuits

конфеты
kanfyety sweets

Бассейн

basseyn The swimming pool

рука
rooka arm

кисть руки
keest' rookee hand

нога
naga leg

20

СТУПНЯ
stoopnya feet

ПАЛЬЦЫ НОГИ
pal'*tsi na***gee** toes

ГОЛОВА
*gala**va*** head

ПОПА
paw*pa* bottom

Раздевалка

razdivalka The changing room

рот
rot mouth

глаза
glaza eyes

уши
ooshi ears

нос
nos nose

волосы
volasy hair

расчёска
*ras**chyos**ka* comb

щётка
***shchyot**ka* brush

Магазин

*mag**azeen*** **The shop**

красный
***kras**niy* red

голубой
*galoo**boy*** blue

зелёный
*zi**lyo**niy* green

жёлтый
*zhol*tiy yellow

розовый
*ro*zaviy pink

белый
*bye*liy white

чёрный
*chor*niy black

Ванная комната *van*naya *kom*nata   The bathroom

мыло
*my*la   soap

полотенце
pala**tyen**tse   towel

туалет
tooa**lyet**   toilet

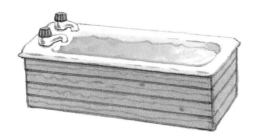

ванна
*van*na   bath

живот
zhi**vot**   tummy

утка
ootka   duck

Спальня   *spal'nya*   The bedroom

кровать
kravat'   bed

лампа
lampa   lamp

окно
akno   window

дверь
dver' door

книга
kneega book

кукла
kookla doll

мишка
meeshka teddy bear

Match the words to the pictures

апельсин	яйцо	яблоко	шапка
apel'**seen**	yay**tso**	**ya**blaka	**shap**ka

банан
*ba**nan***

вилка
veelka

джемпер
djempir

книга
kneega

корова
karova

кошка
koshka

кровать
kravat'

кукла	лампа	майка	машина
kookla	**lam**pa	**mai**ka	ma**shee**na

30

часы	утка	торт	стол
*cha**sy***	***oot**ka*	***tort***	***stol***

собака
*sa**ba**ka*

сапоги
*sapa**gee***

рыба
***ry**ba*

поезд
***po**yest*

окно
*ak**no***

носки
*nas**kee***

нож
nosh

мишка	молоко	мороженое	мяч
***meesh**ka*	*mala**ko***	*ma**ro**zhenaye*	***myach***

Числа

cheesla   Numbers

1 ОДИН

adeen   one

2 ДВА

dva   two

3 ТРИ

tree   three

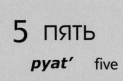

4 четыре

chitirie   four

5 ПЯТЬ

pyat'   five

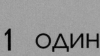

1 ОДИН   **2 ДВА**   **3 ТРИ**   **4 четыре**   **5 ПЯТЬ**

adeen one   *dva* two   *tree* three   *chitirie* four   *pyat'* five